RENAE FULTZ

Leadership: Discovering Your Approach (And Having Fun!)

First edition

This book was professionally typeset on Reedsy.
Find out more at reedsy.com

Contents

1

Introduction

When you begin to think about leadership and are ready to become a leader or refine your current leadership style you are making an investment into your future. This book along with others will be a tool in your leadership tool kit.

I have been a leader since 1992 when I became the President of my dorm floor. The situations I handled as the President of Lancaster House in Willow Hall at Iowa State University were different from those when I was the Vice President at a Fortune 250 company leading an organization of hundreds of employees. While the situations were different I still had most of the same core values. I just did not realize at the time they were my values or how they would guide my leadership style.

These are all topics we are going to dive into in this short book about leadership styles, values, communication, adaptability, and other important topics. This book is not meant to go into great detail regarding each topic but be more of an introduction to leadership and get you thinking.

2

Leadership Styles

First, let's be sure we all understand the differences between a manager and a leader. Are all managers leaders? The answer is yes, all managers are leaders (they may not be good leaders but they are leaders). Are all leaders managers? No, they are not. Are you surprised by this answer? Many people think that all leaders are also managers. Some of the best leaders I have worked with were not managers, they were individual contributors. They had a passion for what they did and what the organization was trying to achieve. They also had a clear road map on what needed to be done, they tailored communication to their audience's preferred style and helped the organization to move forward.

Now, we will look at the definition of a leader and a manager. In an October 26, 2022 article on www.betterup.com, Shonna Waters, Ph.D. defines a leader as someone who:

- Inspires passion in others
- Has a vision and the path to realize it
- Who ensures their team has the support and tools to achieve

their goals

A manager can be defined as:

- Someone who has a team of employees
- Expected to distribute the workload across all team members
- Handle all HR-related tasks or issues such as approving payroll and time off requests, addressing performance issues, hiring and onboarding new team members

Now that we have a better understanding of the characteristics of a leader, we will start to look at the ten traditional leadership styles. It is important to realize your leadership style will be a combination of several styles and will be different based on the situation. For example, most leaders' styles will be different in crisis settings compared to normal day-to-day business. Your leadership style will need to evolve as there are generational differences and changes to social norms and technology. Let's go ahead and dive into the leadership styles.

Autocratic Leadership Style

This leadership style is typically in effect when there is one leader in the organization who makes decisions unilaterally. In this leadership style, there is no collaboration or input from others. Can you imagine the responsibility this leadership style comes with? I like to think two brains are better than one. With an autocratic leader, there is only one decision-maker. Can you think of a scenario where a leader might need to be more autocratic vs. another leadership style? Maybe in an emergency or crisis? There may not be time to involve others in making

3

decisions. The autocratic leadership style would not be popular in today's workforce which values collaboration and providing input. This leadership style stifles creativity, and innovation and ultimately could cause an organization to fail in today's environment.

Democratic Leadership Style

This style is also known as Participative leadership. In this style, leaders are actively asking for input on decisions and soliciting feedback on how to make things better. These leaders are masters at collaborating, they value diversity and believe in empowerment. These leaders want their team members to feel a sense of ownership and responsibility for decisions. The only thing I want to caution you about with this leadership style is it can be time-consuming to get everyone's opinions, and consensus and could delay projects or goals being accomplished.

Laissez-Faire Leadership Style

This is a hands-off leadership style. There is minimal direction provided and team members are expected to be self-motivated. Laissez-faire leaders trust their team members to own all of their tasks and responsibilities. These leaders are not micro-managers and are typically not interested in the specifics of how their team members accomplish their tasks. Can you think of a scenario where this leadership style would be effective? One scenario is when you are working with an experienced, self-motivated team. These individuals should not require much feedback, can be creative, and own their processes and responsibilities. This type of leadership style would not be effective for a relatively new/young team in terms of tenure and skill. Even with an experienced team, you do run the risk of disengagement of the team (even experienced professionals) as most individuals value feedback and use it as a motivator and a way to improve their performance.

Transactional Leadership Style

This leadership style is all about rewards and punishment for achieving predetermined goals. One aspect that is different for this style is there are extremely clear expectations defined right from the beginning. Since bonuses and promotions are based on the established goals this is a very short-term focused leadership style. There is normally a lack of creativity and is very much a traditional hierarchical-based style.

One example where this style would be effective is in a manufacturing plant where the line workers know their goals for various bonus payouts. These workers will decide which level (if there are different levels) and work towards the goal they wish to achieve. They will not be worried about the breakdown of processes or letting others know when the processes are not working, they will simply find a workaround. I want to provide a quick comment about bonuses, it is human nature to never want to put ourselves in peril or feel uncomfortable, as leaders we must do that for them. This means most individuals, if given the choice of three bonuses, will pick the middle one. Our goal as leaders is to provide the confidence and the right tools for our team members to want to reach the highest/hardest bonus level. This is where the next leadership style takes over...

Transformational Leadership Style

As mentioned above, we as leaders, need to assist our team

members in inspiring them to achieve things they never expected were possible. This is the basis of the transformational leadership style. These leaders focus on having a clear vision for the future, communicating the vision, and providing them with the right environment and tools to inspire them to work towards this goal. You might be asking yourself, how do they do this? They purely take an interest in their employees by creating an emotional connection. They know the names of their team members' spouses/partners/significant others and even the names of their pets. They know what their team members are passionate about outside of work and take an interest. This doesn't mean transformational leaders are spending a significant amount of time outside of work with their employees, it just means they know and ask about their lives.

One other key aspect of transformational leaders is that they are typically aware of the needs and development of their team members and provide them with opportunities to achieve this development. This could be something as simple as a weekly training huddle or meeting. Or it could be something more extensive like a one-week development course on project management. Whatever it is, these leaders provide regular development their team is looking for and needs. The final note about this style is these leaders tend to have extremely high ethical standards and are good examples of integrity and accountability.

Charismatic Leadership Style
This style is exactly what it sounds like. These leaders use their charisma to inspire and influence others. They tend to

have a personality that others are drawn to and want to be a part of. These leaders create deep trusting relationships with their team members and can draw others in by having a compelling vision. A charismatic leader has a high level of self-confidence, they are sure of their abilities. One aspect of this leadership style that we have not touched on with many of the others is communication. These leaders tend to be amazing communicators and are usually thought to be storytellers who can draw people into their message. Can you think of some famous leaders who embodied the charismatic leadership style? Steve Jobs comes to my mind along with Martin Luther King Jr.

Servant Leadership Style

In this leadership style, the needs of others are put as the highest priority. A servant leader's primary goal is to serve and support others above their interests or needs. These leaders tend to show empathy, are selfless, and are constantly working to understand the needs of their team members. In this leadership style, listening becomes the focus. Servant leaders want to listen to concerns and ideas and want to be sure their team members feel heard.

One interesting aspect of this leadership style is the long-term focus it has. Listening (and making changes to benefit the team) all help in setting up the team for long-term focus and success. I remember what one high-level executive said to me during a conversation, She measures her success on the impact she has on others. No truer statement could be made about servant leadership. When you are talking to leaders, one way you can determine their primary leadership style is to ask the question, how do you measure your success? Give it a try, you will be amazed at what you will learn about others.

Bureaucratic Leadership Style

As the title of this leadership style might suggest this leader is defined by following rules, procedures, and policies. These leaders tend to fit well within traditional hierarchical organizations. This style of leadership may seem impersonal to team members as there is little focus on personal relationships or qualities. For a bureaucratic leader, they are primarily focused on the efficiency and consistency of their operations. These leaders like predictability, they do not want to deviate from a process that is working and predictable. Can you see any issues with this leadership style? One issue I can see is there is little focus on creativity or process improvement. This leadership style is focused on the short term versus looking to the future at what might be needed.

There are some industries where this style of leadership is needed. I think about the manufacturing of airplanes, or government equipment. Following well-established rules provides safety and security to the country and beyond.

Situational Leadership Style

It may not come as a surprise, that this leadership style is based on the situation. This allows the situational leader to customize their response based on the individuals on the team and the scenario. This particular style is all about adaptability. A few advantages of this style include:

- Encourages the development and growth of followers
- Flexibility to adapt based on the team's skills
- Communication is based on a two-way flow of informa-

8

tion to communicate expectations, provide feedback, and understand the concerns of the team

One of the things I like most about this leadership style is the idea of adapting to the team/followers and the scenario. As a leader, you will be faced with a variety of situations and they all need to be handled differently.

Finding Your Approach

How do you find your approach to leadership? It depends on the organization you are working for and what is needed to achieve the goals. Much of this comes down to the level of tenure/knowledge of the team, the goals of the organization, and some of who you are as a person. Remember your values come through your leadership style. In Chapter Three we will focus on exploring and determining your values.

3

Your Personal Values

L et's start by discussing how your personal values impact your leadership style. What are personal values? These are deeply held beliefs that shape us as individuals in terms of attitudes, choices and behaviors. They really determine how we view right and wrong. What are some examples of personal values?

- Integrity
- Respect
- Responsibility
- Compassion
- Courage
- Equality
- Family
- Creativity
- Learning
- Etc, etc.

I will tell you about my personal values and how they impact my leadership style. My personal values are Responsibility (or accountability), Integrity and Compassion. I lead with a high level of honesty with high standards ensuring that goals and objectives are achieved on time and done the right way while also being mindful of my team and their needs.

Let's use a different example around personal values and your leadership style. For this example, we will use the following values; Equality, Creativity and Family. For this leader they would be sure everyone on their team is equal - everyone has a voice, are respected and included in decision making. They will also be looking for the team to come up with new ideas and not get caught up in the status quo and will be mindful of work life balance, understanding family is important and be flexible with personal obligations.

How do you determine your core values? It is very much a personal journey. There are some ways to understand your values including:

- Make a list of what is important to you and then number them from most important to least important.
- Ask friends and family - sometimes others know us better than we do ourselves.
- Keep a journal and write about why you made various decisions and look for some commonalities.
- Examine some of your past decisions and actions. What was your motivation behind those actions?

One point to keep in mind is that your values will evolve over time. Be patient, your values will become clearer as you are more mindful of them.

4

Communication Preferences

What are communication preferences? This is how you like to receive and provide information. There are several common communication preferences, a few are listed below:

- Verbal vs. Written - Do you prefer to write emails or send information through a message platform or do you like to talk face to face, through video conferencing, etc?
- Direct vs Indirect - Direct in this case is straightforward or do you prefer a more subtle approach?
- Listening vs. Talking - Do you prefer to listen (think servant leadership) or do you prefer to be the one leading the conversation (charismatic leader)?
- Amount of Detail - Some individuals want lots of data and information while others just want to understand the outcome or what you learned compared to the process and details you used.

Let me provide an example. I had the same manager for nearly ten years. While I am someone who wants to understand all of the details, he wanted only a summary and was more focused on the outcome and expected results. I learned I would lose him in the conversation if I tried to go through the details. I tailored my message to only provide what he was looking for. My team knew if they were proposing a change to me, I would ask for the details, and if they did not have the information we would reschedule that conversation to a later time.

It is important to know your communication preferences, it is just as important to understand your audience's preferences. How do you know those preferences? Here are a few ideas:

- Observe them - do they usually send information by email, schedule a meeting, use a messaging platform, etc..
- Ask them directly - this is the easiest way to understand what communication preferences they have, Be prepared though some people do not know their preferences.
- Watch their body language and facial expressions. Non-verbal communication can give you an idea as to how the conversation is perceived by your audience.
- Adapt and test - Try different communication preferences, and determine if are successful - if not, try a different strategy.

Understanding the communication preferences of both yourself and those you work with will ensure more productive outcomes and the overall organization will move quicker.

Different assessments in the marketplace can assist in understanding communication preferences. I have personally used the DiSC assessment and have found it to be accurate and useful. There are some good descriptions of the tool at www.discprofile.com. They describe the tool as a personal assessment tool used by more than one million people every year to help improve teamwork, communication, and productivity in the workplace.

The following information is also provided on the referenced website. DiSC is an acronym that stands for the four main personality profiles described in the DiSC model: (D)ominance, (i)influence, (S)teadiness and (C)onscientiousness.

People with D personalities tend to be confident and place an emphasis on accomplishing bottom-line results.

People with i personalities tend to be more open and place an emphasis on relationships and influencing and persuading others.

People with S personalities tend to be dependable and place an emphasis on cooperation and sincerity.

People with C personalities tend to emphasize quality, accuracy, expertise, and competency.

This is just one example of an assessment you can use to better understand your preferences and those you work with regularly. If the organization you are working for already has an established assessment they use, be sure and embrace this method. I suggest educating yourself regarding the tool/assessment and talking to your team about it. The only way these assessments provide a high level of value is if everyone embraces and uses the results to improve communication, teamwork, etc.

5

Adaptability

C an you imagine going through life with the same ways of thinking and doing things as when you were in kindergarten? I hope you laughed a little at that thought! All of us as human beings evolve and adapt as we go through life. Why is that important as leaders? The Center for Creative Leadership says, "Adaptability is a requirement. Because change is constant and inevitable, leaders must be flexible to succeed."

Let's explore some reasons why adaptability is so important for a leader.

- Today's world is constantly changing and leaders will face unpredictable circumstances. The ability to make adjustments to strategies and plans will allow leaders (and organizations) to be successful.
- There will be the need to quickly adjust to new information, unexpected developments, and any unforeseen circumstances. For example, think of the flexibility it took for leaders of organizations that have had large data breaches.

They could not go with their usual response as this was a new situation that needed to be handled quickly and correctly as it would have large sweeping impacts.

- Leaders will also need to problem solve and alternative solutions will need to be identified to address complex issues. Think about the data breach example I just used.
- In today's business world as technology is evolving and changing an adaptable leader is fostering an environment of creativity along with the willingness to try new ideas to help with continuous improvement.

There are many other reasons why leaders must be adaptable. What are some ways leaders can remain flexible/adaptable?

- Continuous learning - This is when you see obstacles as opportunities for development rather than a problem.
- Stay up-to-date on industry trends and emerging technology. This allows leaders to respond proactively versus playing catch-up and being reactive.
- Change is scary for most people, adaptable leaders embrace change. You should also encourage your team to view change positively.
- Contingency planning is also another way to be an adaptable leader. This is a form of strategic planning and important for an adaptable leader to ensure well-thought-out contingencies are in place.

A strong leader will always need to be adaptable and should be a role model for their team in regards to adaptability. I think sometimes as leaders we forget our team members and others are always observing us. If they see us being adaptable, being open to change, and continually learning while planning for contingencies they will model that same behavior.

6

High-Performing Teams

According to an article on www.leanagility.com, "A high-performing team is a group of people who share a common vision, goals, metrics and who collaborate, challenge, and hold each other accountable to achieve outstanding results."

Let's take that definition and break it down a bit more granular.

- Shared goals and vision - Team members understand the team's goals and are committed to achieving these goals.
- Strong leadership - Provide direction, support, and motivation while empowering team members
- Clear roles and responsibilities - there is clarity around each team member's roles and responsibilities which helps in eliminating overlap and confusion around who is doing what.
- Effective communication - This is for all team members not just the leader. They freely share information, ideas, and feedback (this one is crucial for success).

- Trust among team members - There is a high level of trust, and team members feel safe in sharing information, thoughts, and opinions.
- Collaboration - These teams work together leveraging each team member's strengths to achieve the established goal.
- Accountability - All team members hold themselves accountable for their commitments and overall performance.
- Continuous improvement - there is strategizing improved ways to achieve their goals, they look for feedback and analyze results.
- Resilience - This is when the high-performing team remains focused even when there are setbacks or unforeseen obstacles.

High-performing teams do not just happen overnight. They take time to develop. Here are some steps a leader can take to build and nurture a high-performing team:

- Define clear goals and objectives - set clear, specific, and measurable goals. Ensure everyone understands the team's purpose and the desired outcomes.
- Select the right team members - Choose a group with diverse skills, experience, and perspectives.
- Establish roles and responsibilities - clearly define roles and responsibilities for each team member and how their work contributes to the overall success of the team.
- Promote trust - create an environment where it is safe to share ideas, and concerns without criticism or retaliation.
- Encourage open communication - open and transparent communication is key, the team should listen actively, provide honest feedback, and have regular check-ins on the

progress of the goals.

- Build collaboration - The team should work together, share knowledge, and help each other succeed.
- Set high standards - hold the team accountable to high standards of excellence by instilling a high level of quality and continuous improvement.
- Invest in team development - Provide opportunities for team members to expand their skills and grow personally.
- Create a vision - The vision should be inspiring and motivating to the team members, it is always good to include the team in the creation of the vision.
- Empower decision-making - have team members take ownership of their decisions related to their role that align with the team goals.
- Manage conflict constructively - The leader needs to address conflicts promptly and constructively.
- Celebrate achievements - Recognize and celebrate individual and team successes. One thing to remember is some team members do not appreciate public praise so be mindful of their individual preferences.
- Measure and review performance - compare progress to established goals, and identify any areas where improvement is needed.
- Adapt - encourage the team to adjust their strategies and approaches as needed
- Lead by example - this one is simple, model the behaviors you expect from your team.

The goal of every leader should be to create high-performing teams. These teams are the gold standard and they can accomplish more than most teams in a shorter period. You might be asking yourself, how will I know when my team is high-performing? They are easy to spot, their productivity output is higher than other teams, and is more accurate. They have fun working together celebrate their wins and work to correct any obstacles - all as a team.

7

Setting Goals

T he setting of goals is important for every aspect of our lives. Just one point here, Studies show if you write down your goals, you are more likely to achieve those goals than if you don't write them down. It is also important to revisit those goals regularly after you write them down. It is not just enough to write them down and move on.

How do you set goals? Do you set goals that you know you can achieve or are you on the other side where your goals are so hard you lose interest relatively quickly? In my opinion, setting the right goal is somewhere in the middle of those two. Have you heard of setting a SMART goal? I really like this process of setting goals. Let's dive into what it means.

- S - Specific - your goals should be clear and well-defined. This part of the goal should be what you want to accomplish.
- M - Measurable - this portion allows you to track towards your goals, this will quantifiable or milestone achievements
- A - Achievable - goals should be realistic and attainable,

they should be a reach but not impossible to achieve.
- R - Relevant - goals should align with your long-term plans, they should have significance and relevance.
- T - Time Bound - your goals should have a time frame or deadline.

Let's look at some goal statement examples and determine if they are SMART goals.

- I want to get healthy. While this is a great goal, it needs more components to it. How about - I will lose 15 pounds over the next 5 months. Does this goal meet all of the SMART goal criteria? It's specific, it's measurable, it's achievable, it's relevant since my overall goal is to get healthy and it has a deadline.
- I want to buy a house. This too is a great goal, it also needs some additional components. How about - I will buy a house by the end of 2024. Does this updated goal meet all of the SMART goal criteria? It does, it is specific, it's measurable - I either buy the house or not, it's achievable and it's relevant to my overall goal of wanting to buy a house. You could also add some additional details such as having a certain amount of money for a down payment by a certain date.

The advantage to setting SMART goals is to create a more structured and actionable plan. This will allow you to track your progress which will lead to a higher probability of achieving your goals.

8

Data Analysis

D ata analysis is a broad term and entire full-length
books are written on this topic. For our purposes, we
are going to look at some high-level concepts used
frequently in data analysis.

You may have taken a statistics course and as we go through
a few of these concepts, they may sound familiar!

In an article titled "Type of Data Analysis," they list four types
of data analysis:

- Descriptive - this is the what and shown over time, these are
  what most organizations refer to as a KPI (Key Performance
  Indicator). It might be total expense by month, or it could
  be a % Completion or maybe a variable cost/unit.
- Diagnostic - this is the reason behind the descriptive
  analysis, what is causing the change in the KPI. For example,
  if you own a pizzeria and your cheese cost is high, you might
  look at other information such as the overall cost/lb for
  cheese over time, or maybe the waste % or even the % of
  extra cheese pizzas. All of these will allow you to determine

why your cheese cost was higher.

- Predictive - This is now getting into forecasting and details what is likely to happen. You may start with a sales forecast for the next year and that will then dictate if you need more equipment, people, etc. There are many use cases for predictive data analysis.
- Prescriptive - This is where you take all of the data from the first three and apply it to a problem/decision you need to make and allow the data to determine the solution. In the current business landscape, this is where business intelligence solutions can help (Tableau, PowerBI, etc.) and where the use of artificial intelligence will come into play.

Once you have all of your data analysis complete, how do you summarize it so others can more easily understand it? For this example, we are going to use the first two types of data analysis. We will use the example of owning a pizzeria and having a higher cheese cost.

In the graph below we can see that our cheese cost per pizza has been consistent until May 2023.

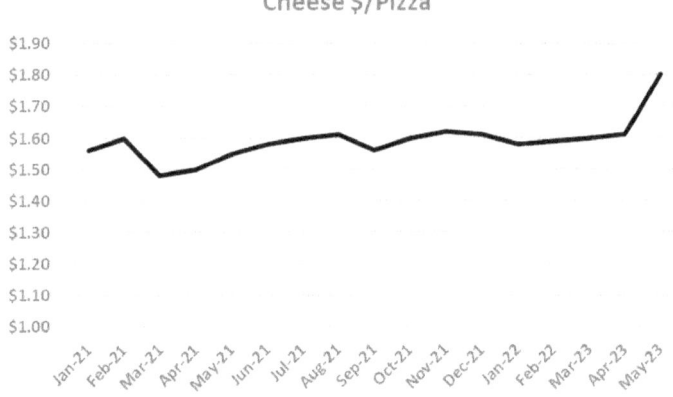

Cheese $/Pizza

Let's explore a few items that could be causing this increase.

- What is the mix of pizza sizes? Did large become a larger % of the total?
- What is the cost per lb for the cheese used in the pizzeria?

First, we will look at the pizza size mix. We are trying to see if large pizzas became a larger % of pizzas sold in May 2023. The graph below shows the pizza size mix.

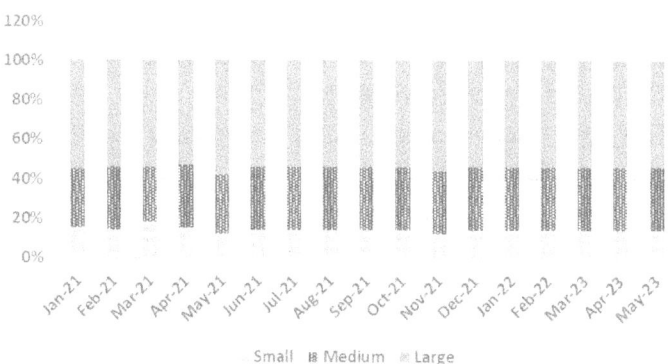

We can see from the graph, that the pizza size mix has been relatively stable over the last seventeen months. Now we need to look at the cheese price/lb.

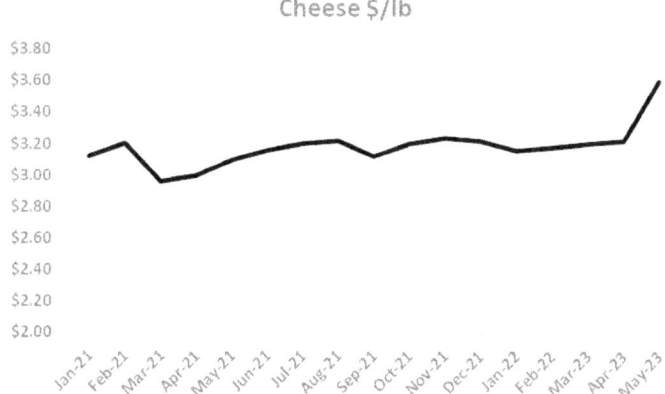

Now we have the cause of what caused our cheese \$/pizza to increase in May of 2023. The cost per lb for cheese (from the pizzeria's supplier) went up causing a corresponding increase in the cheese \$/pizza to increase.

This is just a simple example to understand and start thinking about data analysis.

9

Pulling It All Together

I n this short book we touched on several different topics at a high level. How do you bring it all together and start being the leader you want to be?

First, determine your personal beliefs that will guide you as a leader (and just as your own person). Using those personal beliefs, create your vision of you as a leader thinking about how you want your team to view you. What would they say about you if others asked? If you can determine how you want others to view you as a leader, you will be far on your way to creating a leadership vision.

Once you know all of this, it is a matter of collaborating, communicating, adapting, holding your team accountable and having fun. Yes, that's right, you should be having fun and so should your team. I haven't mentioned the word fun in this book until now, it's very important. When I am leading a team, I tell them frequently, you spend more time at work than at home, it ought to be enjoyable and fun. Not everyday will be full of laughter and fun, but when you look back and you achieved goals you never thought possible, you should say, that was fun.

In the end, having fun while accomplishing great things is what leadership is all about. To do that, you need to be focused on the topics we have discussed in this short guide on leadership.

I wish you all the best in finding your leadership approach... .and having fun! If you enjoyed this book, I hope you will leave a positive review on Amazon.